MORE PRAISE FOR *SO*

Southern Migrant Mixtape surges with color, sound, and emotion. Keeve's juxtaposition of historical and present-day violence creates empathy and a deeper understanding of love and the power of the imagination.

— ROCHELLE SPENCER, author of *AfroSurrealism: The African Diaspora's Surrealist Fiction* (Routledge, 2018)

Vernon Keeve's *Southern Migrant Mixtape* is a beautiful and historic analog move of memory as poems and prose, to record. On his *tracks*, Keeve soulfully, sensually and vulnerably lays down his journey. The storysongs are full of queer ripening and racial awakening, mother tongue and father wit—all at play with the specificity of the colors, sounds, textures, smells and monuments of *the country*. This collection crackles with blackness, queerness, spirit, grit, trauma, surrender, and joy and the distortions of the south. You are left knowing that what is shared, curated by the writer's heart, is dedicated to you and your story.

— MARVIN K. WHITE, author of four collections of poetry including *Our Name Be Witness*; *and last rights*.

SOUTHERN
MIGRANT
MIXTAPE

NOMADIC
PRESS

OAKLAND

2926 FOOTHILL BOULEVARD #1
OAKLAND, CA 94601

2301 TELEGRAPH AVE
OAKLAND, CA 94610

BROOKLYN

475 KENT AVENUE #302
BROOKLYN, NY 11249

WWW.NOMADICPRESS.ORG

MASTHEAD

FOUNDING AND MANAGING EDITOR
J. K. FOWLER

ASSOCIATE EDITOR
MICHAELA MULLIN

DESIGN
BRITTA FITHIAN-ZURN

MISSION STATEMENT

Nomadic Press is a 501 (C)(3) not-for-profit organisation that supports the works of emerging and established writers and artists. Through publications (including translations) and performances, Nomadic Press aims to build community among artists and across disciplines.

SUBMISSIONS

Nomadic Press wholeheartedly accepts unsolicited book manuscripts, as well as pieces for our annual *Nomadic Journal.* To submit your work, please visit: www.nomadicpress.org/submissions

DISTRIBUTION

Orders by trade bookstores and wholesalers: please contact Small Press Distribution, 1341 Seventh Street, Berkeley, CA 94701
spd@spdbooks.org
(510) 524-1668 / (800) 869-7553 (Toll Free)

This book was made possible by a loving community of family and friends, old and new.

For author questions or to book a reading at your bookstore, university/school, or alternative establishment, please send an email to info@nomadicpress.org.

Cover Art by Patricia Atkinson

Published by Nomadic Press, 2926 Foothill Boulevard, Oakland, California, 94601

First printing, 2018

Printed in the United States of America

Southern Migrant Mixtape
p. cm.
Summary: *Southern Migrant Mixtape* relays the experiences and observations of a black, queer man from Virginia who thought he was leaving racism and sexual intolerance behind in the regions where he initially experienced them. Plunge heart first into this emotive journey of growth, transformation of pain into armor, and the lessons that can be learned when one is true to themselves.

[1. Queer. 2. African American.] I. III. Title.

2018932683

ISBN 978-0-9994471-5-4

SOUTHERN MIGRANT MIXTAPE

VERNON KEEVE III

NOMADIC PRESS

TRACK LIST—

SIDE B:

1. FEAR

2. BATTLE HYMN

HOME

This is a town of concrete bridges over waters the shade of loam. In the spring, and in the summer, the shores of that river were, and are, flooded with dense emerald canopies that lean to dip their leaves in the telltale vein of historic conquest—this Rappahannock claim.

At times, the waters will rise and the trees will be ripped from the rhizome of their homes, to become drifting, ignored, and troublesome wood

damming in the concrete columns
of the bridge called Chatham.

The more mammoth and crumbling Falmouth stood—stands— at the bottom of the fall-line, where the rapids grab the most life from the slopes of mud and clay—this bridge bounces from deflection. The currents and rocks north of this bridge could kill you after a storm, or give life to a kayak, but the water on the south side of the bridge is temperate as it snakes its way to the Chesapeake Bay—winding itself to the ocean.

To the north and to the west of those concrete bridges in my town, is the birth of that persuasive river, buried in the back of the serpentine ridges of the Appalachian Mountains.

Trees become wood
that thump against
the legs of bridges—
suppressing the river
altogether.

A slave named John Washington crossed the river to freedom one year before Lincoln proclaimed it, in early spring, 81 years before the Falmouth Bridge was erected.

Rappahannock is derived from an Algonquian word meaning "river of quick, rising water" or "where the tide ebbs and flows." The chief of the tribe after which the river was named cursed the river as his people were being ripped from their taproots.

The waters shrunk and no
longer allowed for the passage of ships.

The river never rises in the winter. Sometimes the edges opal over with ice and frost, and the hollow trees look like withered fingers reaching for a sky of unpolished silver.

That river flooded once, my mother says it flooded all the way to her front porch and into her basement, in the part of town in which she grew up. Crow-foot Bottom, they called it. It was and still is on the other side of the train tracks. Gentrified now. Those old dust-covered wood floors in those southern homes have been polished and varnished to the point which none of the old denizens I met growing up can afford them.

The hundred year flood, mom called it. Happens every hundred years or so, just a really big flood.

I wonder is that flood the equivalent to the big one hitting over here? And, would the big one only affect the homes in West and East Oakland?

fragmented places
spaces for our fears
places where we know they
are tightly confined
to spore rust and decay

amongst them/
       selves

This is a town of church bells, crepe myrtles, and cemeteries. This is a town where the crickets and cicadas lull you to sleep, along with the whirr of the fan to keep the mosquitos away so you can leave the window cracked, even when the air conditioner is running. A town where parents are more concerned with the cost of their energy bills than nurturing the parts of people that hear the music at funerals, see the flowers on top of the graves, ignoring the names on stones.

This is a town where the hydrangeas bloom
in different colors on every block and few
people notice it.

I prefer the blue ones.

This is a town where the queer bar should be frequented on karaoke night, where old friends welcome you with hugs and promises of kinships with longevity, where the schools would never hire me for my effete wrist and tendency to say *Girrrrl*.

This is a town where I feared to be myself,
and yet I've always remained myself;
and even became myself.

On the corner out
side of the courthouse
there's a Color Guard
of stars and stripes
spinning their plots
above their heads.

Their songs and chants fall,

withered petals onto graves trodden
black.

Richard and Mildred Loving,
the denouement of the
rebel's yell.

The courthouse is large with a steeple like a church, like the churches
two, three, and four blocks away from it. Three of those churches
on Sundays fill to the brim with black faces that sing from a hymnal
that blends sacred hymns with music once sung in fields—

filling white pages with black measures,
filling black measures with black notes,
and linking black notes to form black chords—
chords enumerated a freedom that could never be
felt.

A religion fed to us in the bonds of spiritual starvation from what
was sacred to our black faces. The eradication of our own truth, and
yet we don't fly flags with coiled snakes, nor do we have a symbol
of our rebellion that flying above our heads. What if I flew a flag
with Nat Turner on it? Would they relate him to the snake or the
rebel, which have become one in a town of forgotten histories,
surrounded by battlefields. General Lee is all over this place. Kunta
Kinte is rarely spoken about, even though he was murdered on the
grounds where the battlefield birthed a courthouse. Not too far
from the grounds where many of the deputies still dress in costumes
to remember that it is a heritage thing, and they lie to themselves
whenever they put cuffs on brown wrists.

They will never call these cuffs shackles, just like they will never call their heritage hate, or maybe they do in the privacy of their homogenous friendships and homes with fences and white hydrangeas. An ignorance of their own blindness. A confederation of collusion and with the freedom to express it.

They will never understand the chants from mothers with calloused hands that were never allowed to touch their children with cotton-soft fingers. They will forever feel like the snake under the heel— treaded upon.

They will never welcome me to tea, and I will never understand their fictional slave narrative.
A nickel that white faces would offer black children
five pennies to pose on the slave auction block
for photos
that was in the '60's
when pieces of candy costs the fraction of a penny
two bit o honey's for a penny
or three gumballs
Mama recalls

A nickel for a picture that would end up in photo albums, next to photos of the tomb of the unknown soldier, Ferry Farm, or Mary Washington's house after fame came to her, all because her son was allowed to live.

I watched two white girls play on that auction block, recently, ignoring the plaque of recognition, mother too busy exiting the butcher shop with grass-fed meat to explain history.

She pulls them off the block, un-phased by the horror.
A distant cousin attempted to destroy it in his teens. A graduate
from my alma mater tried to destroy it in the '90s, but the stone will
not be moved. Ignored by those unaffected—those of the side of
history that looked up into the face of the merchandise—the meat
before the market.

Those that had spare nickels, and pennies to throw away.

I remember singing "Shenandoah" in district chorus. The image of
a river cutting through a valley made me reach for the high notes,
but the truth of the region allowed me to hit the low notes with
no problem. I sang tenor, but I felt the heavy darkness of the bass
everyday.

I remember learning the word *whitewash* in middle school. It was
one of our vocabulary words. I remember looking up antonyms,
words like *stain*, *mar*, and oddly, *expose*.

If I used *blackwashing* in a sentence, what image does it bring to
mind. My teacher used the example of a man painting a fence white
to relay the meaning of whitewashing into our developing minds.
When I say *blackwashing*, do you think of a man painting a fence
black? Does something more sinister come to mind?

The now urbanized fence will not be crossed by many. Others will
ignore it for the land that providence told them was theirs. The
fence does not exist when it is painted black. What color is your
imagined picket fence?

This is a town where the train station is central and frequented by the government workers who cannot speak of their jobs. Where coffee warms the hands of those waiting to hear the arrival bell—a town of early mornings and mourning doves. This is a town with one of the last concrete bridges in America. A town of arches and columns.

This is a town of moms and pops, and the children that choose to keep them alive. A town with shops that have flimsy doors with fragile locks and no alarms. A town where one can leave their bike unattended and unlocked while they run in

to.

A town where lifted trucks are feared by blacks
more than whites fear
those on the other side of the train tracks
upon which I just departed.

unshackled son
sets in the west
left the south with

a next step

thought the rocky coast
would allow him to catch
his breath, but son still
runs away from the night

son still caught up
in the native fight

You are both of
my body, your words
gave narrative to

my body,

but when this
queer black boy
needed Coat(es)
you did not warm
this Citizen.

The fabric was laid
like the lore that gave
your books spaces on shelves
and ignored like the unread.

I felt the ode to my pigment
lead to an endless segue and the choir
director was not allowed to move
how he wanted, so he fell to his
knees at and emptied altar
and cried,

leaving a part of himself where caskets
are placed for funerals.

By Baldwin and Rustin and Walker
by Hemphill, Smith comma Barbara,
Cornwell comma Anita,
Hansberry and my Lorde,

Lorde, Lorde,
Lorde, have mercy
on me.

Oak trees in California are different than the Oak trees in Virginia. The trees back home grow high into the sky—much the opposite of their low, crawling cousin, the California Oak. They are both live, dropping no leaves in winter—that is to say that California has a winter.

I once read Thoreau at the University of Virginia, fell in love with nature, wanting to find refuge in places surrounded by cliffs and pines, but then I grew to observe my life in the south. The locations where my family did not travel, and the conversations that trailed the mention of places west of Charlottesville, Virginia, and into the Blue Ridge Mountains.

I attended UVA exactly one decade before Martese Johnson was brutally beaten by ABC officers. I stayed at the prestigious university for one year, after two people on separate occasions were called racial epithets, and both times the campus divided racially—or should I say the division became prevalent, because when I was accepted there was still a separate admissions office for African-American students. BST, or Black Study Time, was when many black students met in Clemons Library to study amongst a similitude of faces. BET, Black Eating Time, was when blacks ate together.

We were made into a horde, and the word *horde* comes with a subtext of opposition.

With all that in mind, I never understood why my father turned the destruction of my car window into a gay *thing* and not a racial *thing*.

"Do you bring your lovers home? Maybe someone saw you bring a lover home."

(It couldn't have had anything to do with my race.)
I left before I could find out, and before my voice disappeared behind the wall of students who didn't look like me. When the black students convened for our granted times together, it looked like there were so many of us, but in class I felt washed out.

I have only encountered Thoreau a few times since then; these days I think of Toni Morrison when I think of nature and literature. The way she weaves the entirety of the black experience into a single telling of lore, her words I will relay to my children, instead of tales that only speak of the magic to be found in nature.

The uncertainty of nature,
the difference in the meaning of *tree*.

Ropes don't grow from
trees like they used to, but
bullets do
splay
like
seeds.

Many dogs still only bark at black faces, and I have inherited the
fear from my ancestors, who were sold as meat and then turned into
meat for dogs as they ran to escape, the same fairy tale that Michael
Brown ran towards even though he knew the truth shot faster than
his steps—there is no magic.

I had driven through the Appalachian Mountains alone once on
a trip to visit a friend in Carmichaels, Pennsylvania. Her mother
white; her father black. And she, a twin. After I drove through the
red covered bridge in Carmichaels to get to her mother's house, she
told me:

with you, my sister, and me here,
there are exactly two black people in town.

We laughed.

There is a dis-
ease in the people
that floods cells
with water

tears down
walls dis-
rupting life, even
stopping it all
together.

While I was there, a man pissed on a tree in her mother's yard. None
of us knew what it meant, but the howl of what I assumed to be
wolves kept me up all night. When I drove back home, I did not stop
in southwestern Pennsylvania, or northeastern West Virginia for
gasoline. And I rediscovered religion when my gaslight came on in
the western part of Virginia, still afraid to stop but closer to home.

There is a dis-
ease in the land
that builds walls
as tears stream
down
bricks from people
trying to climb
over to the other side

Barack Obama was nearing his first win into the white house, and my friend Chris asked me to go camping with him, his mother, and her boyfriend. I did not care for Chris's mom's boyfriend, because he was an NRA member—that is what we call Republicans in the rural south. Correction—that is what we call Republicans everywhere. However, the NRA member, had access to spelunking grounds and the land on which we were camping was behind a gate with lock and key.

There is a disease
in the body
that separates meat
from bone.

I agreed to go, because I had fallen in love with mountains as a naïve child, and because I knew what it was like to be in a mountainous region as a black person, especially as the infamous, fear-mongering black male. I went because my blackness was going to be behind a lock and a key.

I left my "Barack the Vote" shirt at home, along with my true sentiments of Chris' mom's boyfriend.

After we passed Charlottesville into the foothills, the elevation rose as we went westward. Then the car descended into the Shenandoah Valley, then began to lift again, not even an hour later into higher elevations than the previous older and more eroded ridge. We were surrounded on all sides by the George Washington and Jefferson National Forests, rock deformations, societal deformations, and inside of forests named after slaveholders.

Forests with histories of dogs
and runaways, runners, believers
that either made it or didn't.

Roads full of men who draw guns
and become dogs that America has trained
to pull the trigger
when rap music is too loud
for fragility of glass.

The car came to a halt and Chris woke me up from a nap.

He immediately asked me, "What do you want from the store?"
I lethargically began to list what I wanted, before I said, "I'll just go
in."

"Nah dog, don't worry about it. I got you." He promoted my
continuation of sleep, and I wanted to allow it.

"But, I want stuff for the whole weekend, so I'll just get it." I fought
sleep.

"Dog, I just don't think you want to go in there." Chris pointed.
Confederate flags flew over the side of the building painted with the
words NO BAMA.[1]

Chris got me everything I wanted from the store, and I remember as
I write this that I never paid him back—and he never asked me to.

---

[1] I still can't help but to wonder how the storeowner would have treated me.

That store, and the serpentine road that I would've thought was beautiful, was the last thing I saw before going behind the gate of the spelunking grounds, and before being locked in.

I spent the entire Labor Day weekend afraid of being seen. I heard, from the tent, what I assumed to be wolves. Chris informed me that they were just coyotes, and that they would not come near, that they were more afraid of us and fire than we were of them. But every time I heard a truck on the road, I felt like Emmett Till when Roy Bryant knocked on his uncle's door. Images of men peeing on trees kept me awake, dogs marking their territory, looking for runaways, runaways from urban areas—from the concrete prisons of being surveilled.

They sent the dogs into the trees
to bite and rip at the knees
of those who tried to reach the other-
side of the wilderness—

don't be mad when I say lore
told me to fear the pack, but to
fear the hands that freed the dogs
even more.

His spine
was severed

by those
who protect
and serve
a system

that did not
care what was
in his head.

Revolutionaries
are being called
thugs.

When whites did this
they called it
occupy.

Excuse us while we
occupy ourselves.

Black women have never stopped singing
for black men.

Black women have never stopped singing
for themselves.

Shug Avery taught me that.

So many tombstones, marches, murders
and hashtags for a movement that never stopped
moving,

can't afford to stop moving.

Wives, mothers, and daughters crying for:

Eric Garner
Walter Scott
Darrien Hunt
Tamir Rice
…

#somanyblackboysandmenkilledbycopsthatIhavetroublekeepingup-
withallofthenames

All of those sons, brothers, and fathers re-
placed with rap sheets and assumptive guilt—
feigned relation to Cain.

All singin' songs sung by our ancestors
in fields when trees grew strange fruit and

dogs returned with its juice dripping
from their mouths.

The lynchings never died,
only Ida B. Wells and the retelling
of it.

Until the news was spread
by hands that knew the power of hashtags
to become movements.

For those singers of spiritual code
who knew how to follow the drinking gourd,
knew how to swing low,
and wade in the water.

Mamie Till said you could smell
her son's decomposing body
from miles away in the uninterrupted heat
of a 1955 Indian Summer.

When she forced America
to open the casket and see
what it had done to her baby

The decomposition of Emmett is still
happening.

#usedtobemyname

Nature was stolen from us
first and foremost. Black codes
after freedom came

reminded us that there were still
gnashing jaws hidden
amongst the canopies of trees.

So blacks moved to cities, where trees were stolen from us—nature
stolen from us--and we were too afraid of the branches from those
southern species to notice that the green of our surroundings had
been taken from us like Black Wall Street.[2]

There is a dis-
ease in the land.

When I lived in West Oakland I had to cross a highway in all four
directions to get out. There were and are studies being done on the
number of children in West and East Oakland being born with, and
developing asthma—it's an epidemic.

There is a disease in the land.

---

[2] Also known as the Tulsa Race Riot of 1921, when white mobs began attacking
African-American residents—an attack carried out on the ground and via airplanes—
destroying the wealthiest black community in the nation at the time.

The West Oakland Project:
Section 80.

Walled in by-way
the world outside of the barriers
drying out. The body
is now pulling water from
the cell. The highway is no
longer dividing.

Let's proleterrify Oakland.

Let's put a rose garden
in every neighborhood.

Trees for every yard,
yards for every home,
homes for every person.

The highways, divisions of race and class, are more pronounced in Los Angeles. Asthma really hasn't affected me since grade school. There was need to request an inhaler during bouts of whooping cough when I first moved to the damp of the Bay, but asthma still was a tamed beast.

In LA, I could not even sleep with my window open. Every street had cars on them at all times, and there were moments when these cars formed the serpent of Los Angeles—the sipper of oil—the silencer of the river—the breather of smog.

I was surrounded by Latin-Americans of all kinds, and I followed their foodways of buying filtered water from water stations. I ignored the purchasing of water at first, but I knew two weeks after moving into my apartment that kettles were not supposed to develop crystalline chlorine deposits that quickly.
In Los Angeles, there are
so many bodies in the streets
that I forgot they were in cars.

The LA river is a hard vein
that can take no more substance
abuse. No more detritus of man,
his imposing thoughts—
man penetrated the mud and
patriarchy sprouted a poison
US fruit.

Cities are built on swamps:
state-unified legion. We drink
the oil that we will soon become.

We sink, feels good when it's warm.
Pray we dead before scorching.

So many names—most of them boys,[3]
from a timeline in the wilderness,
from lesson in scorching.

Are we still in Canaan,
I see an orchard and in it
are trees, but all of them

saplings, looking towards
fruit; however, the logger only
sees trees.

They will stop killing black boys when we have all been tilled. When
we have all been turned into paper,

to be burned before
it is ever written upon.

Trees torn down to be balled into incomplete ideas and splayed into
piles to be buried. America does not know the true definition of
recycle.

Cement dries without our footprints
though within it dripped our ancestors sweat
tears in the mortar, unseen
blood dried into brick.

Trees that give oxygen are the same ones that made me think of
nooses when Eric Garner said that he could not breathe, but the
suffocation is coming as highways around neighborhoods, bullets

---

[3] There were four girls.

instead of questioning, and the lack of rose gardens in spaces where people deserve them—

only on their graves.

This is why I prefer the gaze of nature through the eyes of black writers. I can't go into flats along the Central Valley, most parts of Virginia, many places in between, and ignore the collective stares towards my black and queer body. Nor ignore the gun-racks that tell me, along with news headlines, that my life could be taken and my killer could walk freely on grounds that were never mine to begin with.

Where can a queer black body go in nature and not fear
the evolution of the Klan? Definitely not Castro Valley or
Charlottesville, or to the cops in San Francisco. We still know that
there are dogs out there pissing on trees and gnawing at knees.

There is a dis-
ease in the land.

Were we ever free?

A southern cotton-
wood grows in my back-
yard, and cotton would make
a bird sing songs
about trees

in a cage.

Are you afraid of the dark-
ness beyond the water? Those
lands drawn from borders and
imagined nations kept secret
by monsters of the sea.

Are you afraid of the dark-
some savage with stone dry
bone through his nose,
a pot boiling with the soup
of the wanderer?

My family was out shopping in Williamsburg, Virginia, and I had on a baby blue Tommy Hilfiger cotton canvas jacket. I was a heavy kid, there was a lot of walking involved that day, and I was getting hot.

To this day I hate carrying a jacket in my hands.
Jackets are meant to be worn.

It always seemed so awkward to carry a jacket in my hands—still does.

Hands should only be filled with their purpose,
and a jacket's purpose is not to warm or fill your
hands.

I let it fall from my shoulders, down my arms, and it rests within the crooks of my bent elbows—much like a fine lady does with a long scarf of many colors—much like Oda Mae Brown in *Ghost*—I've always wanted to be clairvoyant.

I was comfortable, but the fashion created a discourse around my body as if it did not have a conscience. A discourse in which I was subject—the subject that sparked rage in my father, concern in my mother, and fear in myself.

The wind blows blue the Sunday away.

Don't you remember that day when
the screen door slammed over and over?

The wind blew blue that day.

No one fastened the hook,
so that flimsy door
tried to fly with one wing.

It tried.

Screens show no pain,
but the panes in the windows
rattled.

And the rattle is what I remember
most.

"Take your jacket off, or hold it in your hands."

"Why? I'm hot, and if I hold it I might lose it."

I was always setting down things and walking away from them as a child. I picked up the flute in first grade, put it down, my father raged about having to cancel lessons. I do not understand why he was mad. The flute was by his definition a punk instrument—and not punk as in colonialist rock.

I picked up baseball in 8th grade—still heavy—not the best runner, but I hit every ball.

"That fat faggot is terrible," was the last thing I heard at that first practice. I never went back. The coach begged me back two days later, said I could have been a hitter.

"I don't think your team wants me around."

My dad begged me to go back too, but I couldn't use that line with him and with the same implications in my locking of eyes as I did with the coach, and my emphasis on certain words. The coach understood, because like I said, I hit every ball. I would've loved to be a hitter.

"Then pull the jacket up on your shoulders." My father was adamant, and getting visibly frustrated in the middle of the outlet store, and people were beginning to stare.

"Baby, give me your jacket," my mom chimed in.

"No, he can carry it."

"But, I'm comfortable … this way."

"It looks feminine."

"But, I'm comfortable … this way."

"You look like a sissy, and I ain't raising no bitch."[4]

My mother ended up carrying the jacket, my father did not speak to me for the rest of the day, and that is when it happened. The moment when the mouth of my parent removed me from that space amongst the family and placed me in the crowded hallway of my middle school, on a day when my best friend had stayed home sick.

See, I was never allowed a closet door—I had a beaded curtain—and I was made to feel ashamed for it. I was called a faggot before I knew the definition of the word. I was told that I talked like a girl, that I walked like a girl, and that I did things that girls did. Needless to say, all of my friends were girls, and my father asked me often, which one was my girlfriend, up until the day when he got frustrated with

---

[4] "Raisin' No Bitch" is an old time negro spiritual that is still sung—given to us when they took the skirts from our warriors:

> Raisin' no bitch
> I ain't raisin' no bitch
> by everythin' taken from me
> I ain't raisin' no bitch
>
> He don't have to kiss that breeder
> woman on the lips, but
> I ain't raisin' no bitch

the silence that was my closet door, and forced me to speak.

I kept the name-calling and bullying to myself. I kept the names
and the assumptions to myself, because I thought mentioning them
would be a revelation to my parents. If my peers were enforcing
something that they were already trying so hard to ignore, then it
would only validate their unspoken thoughts.

Does every queer child grow up feeling like their parents belong
more to their heterosexual siblings than them?

Loneliness was my best friend until I grew to fear it.

I was never spoken to about the birds and the bees. I don't know the metaphor, or what each one represents, nor will I Google it, but I have assumed what the signifiers stood for over time, and why I wasn't spoken to about sex between men and women, because it would have been a dis-ease for my father. He would have only lashed out in anger. That was the only language we spoke for a long time. Like that spring evening during my sophomore year in college when he called me and blatantly asked me:

"*What* do you sleep with?"

I am a man that has never heard the story of the birds and the bees, so I can only tell you the problems that can arise when queer adolescents are not warned about the hooked beaks belonging to birds of prey, or which bees have stingers, or why the mention of bees when most stings come from yellow jackets. Does the birds and bees discussion mention loving yourself first?

In Fredericksburg, Virginia, the only option of meeting another queer person, in my teenage mind, seemed to be online—America Online to be exact. I didn't mind it at first, because I wasn't all too open with my sexuality at 16, anyway, online felt safe for my curiosities.

My learner's permit had evolved into a provisional license, and the hand-me-down "first car" of the household was all mine. And it was red like my desires at that time, because the only thing I wanted to do with my newfound fresh-faced freedom was to be naked, and with another man.

I was once very ashamed to say that this guy and I did not talk for very long before deciding to meet and have sex. I'm not anymore. I was 16. I smoked three Black & Milds, because I thought it was the cool and appropriate thing to do. I threw up for 23 minutes straight. I remember because it was exactly 10 p.m. when I first leaned over to hurl, and when I looked back up from the pavement, the clock in the car read 10:23 pm. I also started taking diet pills when I was 16, stealing them from the local Wal-Mart. At first, because my friends and I were getting addicted to speed, and then with more incentive when I noticed they curbed my appetite and allowed me to drop from 217 lbs to 150 lbs in one summer.

This guy and I talked online for a week and arranged for me to pick him up after football practice, go to his empty house, and have sex. I should have known when I saw the Dixie Outfitters shirt— Confederate flags crossed—his Southern pride expressed— I should've turned around; however, the South is strange. Some wear this flag in true ignorance, awaiting a life-changing lesson from a person of color, and some like me are completely ignorant of the language that is spoken in households of those that adorn themselves with the flag. He was clearly looking for a lesson from a black male, and he played football; so I was sure his associations with black males were pretty high (as fucked up as that sounds).

I did not know what I was to him, nor did I care. I was not thinking with my brain, and there was a buff football player sitting in my passenger seat. I can still smell him at times, but I could not tell you his name—something I made myself forget. There were many names I should have forgotten, and yet I catch them in my contacts when I get a new phone, and have to download my old contacts all over again.

Sometimes it takes until I've had that perfect day, and I'm riding on the AC transit home, and I'm feeling overly confident in my day's work, to finally assemble the courage to delete those numbers that belong to names that once made me hate my own.

His was the first name I forced myself to delete. We held hands in my car. He explored my body as I drove deeper into the wilds of Spotsylvania County. The Orange County border was visible from his house, a place that was historically infamous for the treatment of its black residents. Hell, Spotsylvania's history is no better, but it was a few miles closer to home.

We made out in the car, before going into his house. We went straight to his room and closed the door. I left with plans to see him again. I drove home listening to the *Parachutes* (back when Coldplay was good)—drifting from that moment on a high that I thought was more than lust.

AOL Instant Messenger greetings went ignored for days, until strangely enough his girlfriend (or someone claiming to be his girlfriend) messaged me saying that I was just his *nigger* experience.

An experience between two people
remains between two people, even if one
of them denies it. Erasure of an orgasm
we both shared, and I am forced to re-
member from time to time.
I can't help but to wonder
as I write this what life
has taught him.

My father and I did not talk to one another for four years.

He initiated a dialogue after Michael Sam revealed to the National Football League that he was a homosexual. With that revelation, and all of the press he received, my dad had stumbled into the language used surrounding Michael Sam in the barbershops, amongst his church's congregation, and his friends. And it clicked.

He understood in those moments that life for me was no *crystal stair*. He understood there is no choice about whom one is attracted to, just like it isn't one's choice to get harassed. Just like I know there is only one choice when I think to ask him about his treatment towards me as a child, or why I don't know about the birds and the bees. I just cannot bring it up when we talk on the phone, because those four years of silence were more painful than any name I have ever been called.

It is a dis-ease for me.

When I was young my mother always had some version of a Jeep Cherokee. There always existed that cargo area that I remember wanting to sit in at all times. It was like a permanent fort in the car, and it seemed ideal for long trips. To nap in, to color in, to play in with my Ninja Turtles. My sisters and I called that space the *way way back*—always with the extra emphasis on the second *waaay*—elongating the word with a youthful chorus. We used to pile groceries in the *way way back*, sometimes with my grandmother sitting in the front of the car talking about one of her neighbors in "the bottom" smoking too much, drinking too much, or helping her out when she needed a friend. We used to pile luggage in the *way way back*, preparing for those 12-hour road trips to Disney World. And we piled boxes and mini fridges in the *way way back* as we all moved from the home we knew to the dorm rooms that separated us. But there was always a way back to welcome our things when the world sent us home for more lessons to be learned. I miss the way way waaay back.

Crows don't talk to me, neither do apes.
Black faces scare me, because I am brown.

Crows don't talk to me.
Apes look at me with alien eyes.

My mother cries because she never learned to swim.

Her brown history is her own. And that of her children.

And, crows don't talk to her either.

When I was 13 years old, I went looking for something. The house
in which I grew up, solely my father's house now, has many cabinets,
many places where things go to be forgotten. I remember going into
the den and opening the cabinet doors. I still have yet to see doors
like those anywhere else. Redwood frames, with stretched cotton
cloth where there should've been a glass pane. They were delicate,
so a brass cross-hatching overlaid both sides of the cloth, to keep
unwanted hands from

touching the pure white canvas,
pulled cotton between the red-
wood frames. No stain in all
those years—no rips nor tears.

Since I was younger than 13, I have had a habit of, and strongly
remember, waving them back in forth on their hinges; because the
fabric in the wind sounded like the blades of the helicopters landing
in those movies that my parents loved to watch, in which some
young man came home from Vietnam[5] too doped up on the truth to
sanely function amongst the lies of the everyday. There was nothing
post- about the traumatic stress of the black men that came home
after war, nor was there anything post-traumatic about the ones who
escaped the draft and still show signs of PTSD.
I went searching inside those descending helicopter blades one day,
and found a sketchbook. In it, was a ballet of pastel flowers dancing
to music from the record player that I only recall hearing once.
Page after page of gardens better than Claude Monet's—a purse of
art I assumed my middle sister had drawn—by mouth of the "bill
payer," she was the only recognized artist in the house, and it just so
happens, her name is Monet.

---

[5] Dead Presidents

The smell of honey-
suckle translates to memory,
a sweetness of moments.

Mama showed us how to
pull the nectar from the receptacle,
memory from her child-
hood.

They grew 'round
the edge of the yard, covered
the ivy in spring.

Mama showed us to savor
them once and we took it
from there. Mama taught us
moments like those.

"No, they're Mama's." The first time my life exploded with the possibility of endless possibility. I was 13, and just finding out that my mother was, and still is, an artist. Her song overlaid by descending helicopter blades, her canvas cross-hatched in a brass overlay.

The wind blew blue that day.

"She got a full ride to the Art Institute of D.C., but got pregnant with Shatema." My mother always got home before my dad. I confronted her with the garden in my hand. I remember the glare on her glasses as she lowered her head, and started preparing dinner.

"What about it?" was something my mother said when she didn't want to talk about something. I stopped pushing the subject when I heard my father's Cole Haan's on the rocky patio, announcing his arrival home from work, which often came with a mood. Being a lawyer in the south dealing with good ol' boys, having flashbacks of the integration of your grade school, being one of the first blacks accepted into a law school on a campus that is a decoration for a country club, and surrounded by old money—pockets still lined with cotton.

All of the walls in his house were white and beige. I stopped to think that my mother named my sister after an artist, that my mother introduced us to all of the magic of Crayola, and did all of our science projects—which were always lauded for their craftsmanship and creativity.

My mother's name is Iris, her mother's Lillie. I put the chorus of pastel flowers back into the chamber of descending helicopter

blades. It probably still rests there, untouched, though my mother
sleeps across town, in her own house, now.

Her living room is sunflower yellow,
and her bedroom is chartreuse.

She has not started drawing again,
but she has rooms to fill—
with color.

The Color Purple plays
like a soundtrack.
Revolutions in fields
of indigo. Taking back
the blues for tunes
that you can swing your
hips to. "Oh Miss Ce-
lie, I feel like singin'."
Your sister stood in
golden fields while you
felt the thorns of roses
that were never meant
for you. You read books
for paper cuts. You made
pancakes for butter and
syrup. They called you
Precious and made you
a mother. "Oh Miss Ce-
lie, I feel like singin'."
Written to serve
the product,
that slave-
ry maid. Written to
tell the story of a woman
made to live on mind
crafted pages.
The forgotten stages
of the primary colors,
that made the color
purple true. The veri-
ty of red and blue.

The remembrance
of those his-
story stained faces.
"Oh Miss Celie, I feel
like singin'."
The Epistles of Celie:
the unmade album.

The wind blew blue that day.

My mother introduced me to my spirit. I do not know how she did it, but she did it. It could have been her waking up an hour before me and my sisters on school days to prepare breakfast, or laying out our clothes, or taking us to school herself before she, herself, went on to work. Or it could have been her leaving work to pick us up from school, dropping us off at home with only two chores of pulling meat out of the freezer, which she would prepare when she returned home after the remainder of her work day, and doing our homework.

In school for 13 years, and I can probably count on my fingers and toes how many times I ate school lunch, because I rarely left home without a brown paper bag—the brown bag my mother's skin was lighter than in the '50s and '60s—the bag that she decorated with my name and messages of encouragement—messages I tried my best to hide as I got older and more anxious about the opinions of others. The only paper bag test I had to pass was to see if it successfully held the lunch that my mother filled it with.

It could have been her taking us to church, or taking off when we were sick (and even faking sick). Her willingness to lose sleep when I woke up with asthma attacks, or after wetting the bed, or just thinking there was something ominous in the closet. It could've been her undying support and longing to understand her children even when we introduced her to issues that she never had to endure.

Or maybe she was introduced to my spirit early in life, before I even had a physical body, before she had met my father.

My mother saw a ghost. One of those days after she picked me up from school, dropped me off at home, and went back to work. Tired and sitting in traffic that did not used to exist in in the City of

Battlefields. Luckily, there was a back entrance to the subdivision that my mother and father worked hard to afford for us—the only black family in the neighborhood—the family in the house next to where they erected the neighborhood watch sign.

A back entrance just on the south side of Blue and Gray Parkway—Gray for the South and Blue for the North. An entrance, or an exit, right next to the cannon that was used by the South, and from which I heard fire every night shortly after 1 a.m. (my mother assured me it was coming from the Dahlgren naval base 30 miles away). I never believed her.

Maybe questioning beyond the woman that gave me life, questioning beyond the woman who would clip her own roots to make sure her seeds were watered, introduced me to my spirit.

The Battle of Fredericksburg lasted for four days, December 11–15, in the '60s, 1862 to be exact. The South lost 608 men on that day; the North, almost 1300. And even though more northern blood was shed, it was a gray coat that my mother saw on her way home on that particular day that she saw that particular ghost, crossing the road with his head bowed, walking in a disillusioned state. "He looked lost, and wanted to be acknowledged," I recall her saying. Even before this incident, my mother had seen ghosts. The first account she shared happened in the very office from which she came, the office that was my father's law office, the office that used to be her childhood dentist's office. Sitting in her desk positioned next to a window facing the driveway, she would see the old, olive green Cadillac of the deceased Dr. Wyatt pull up—the car she remembered from her childhood, park, and disappear, but only after she would hear the wooden screen door in the back slowly creak open and quickly slam shut.

She never feared him. Why her? Why hadn't my father encountered the ghost? He ventured into the stone cellar—where the dentist stored his equipment before he died and where his equipment still rusts—more than my mother, and he never encountered the ghost of the wandering toothsman. He stayed behind well into the night sometimes and had never mentioned any weird happenings.

My mother introduced me to my spirit.

My mother spoke to the ghost of the dentist one day after she saw his Cadillac and heard the door slam, saying "Dr. Wyatt, you may not remember me, but you used to be my dentist when I was a little girl. You can stop scaring me now. It's time to move on." And with that she never saw the phantom Cadillac pull up again, nor did she hear that door slam again.

My mother slowed down when she saw the gray coat. When I was a kid my mother used to pick up children she saw walking to school as she took us. One time the kids she picked up didn't even go to my school, and she still went out of her way to drop them off. She would also pick up people she knew from her childhood, if she saw them walking along the road. I don't know if my mother thought the gray coat was in distress, or looked familiar even, but she slowed down; and when she did, he crossed the road before her.

He wanted to be acknowledged by her like those many times she saw her father right after he died, and before she married my dad. He walked across the road slowly, before her stopped car, and disappeared when he got to the other side, marching from the trenches on the south side of the road to those on the northern side. As if my mother were a bridge leading wanderers across a raging, white river—the bridge that carried me from the darkness to the light. The bridge that introduced me to my spirit.

The house she lives in now is a house that she had always wanted. She walked past it as a child on her way to church, imagining it painted yellow. My father purchased it as a rental property after it caught on fire and needed to be gutted and renovated in the '90s—my mother's suggestion. When they divorced she was given the house, not the office that had been cleansed and became a rental property after my father purchased the office he uses today, but the house that she always wanted.

The builder of that house, and many of the houses surrounding it, lived in the house my mother lives in. Her garage is his old workshop. Filled with his old tools, old Campbell's soup cans, matches and Lucky Strike boxes. In the summer when the grass grows high, the pathway leading to his workshop appears trodden as if he still uses it.

One summer when I go to visit her, the grass will probably be sprouting and growing tall along that historic pathway, blending into the yard, and she will have another story to tell me.

My mother, the bridge.

My mother introduced me
to my spirit.

unfried unwashed
potatoes rest-
ing in a paper sack
on the porcelain farm-

house drain-
board sink,

empty cake keepers,
unslammed storm doors
on springs. differing spigots

separating hot from cold, un-
fried unwashed
potatoes rest-
ing in a paper sack
on the porcelain farm-

house drain-
board sink,

empty cake keepers,
unslammed storm doors
on springs. differing spigots

separating hot from cold,
unhugged. my Nannie

used to live
here

My maternal grandmother was born in 1933 in Spotsylvania,
Virginia. She lost the pinky on her right hand as a little girl because
she held out her hand to grab a boy who whizzed by on a bike. He
got away with more than her heart that day. She was taught that
white mouths held all truths, so she prayed until her skin faded
in places. She became lighter than those mouths in places, but her
mouth stayed brown around the edges, most of her hands stayed
brown, and those hands that cleaned a school board office where
her symmetrical spots on her skin were the darkest pigment in
the building until the integrating class came back from college
and enforced change, and even then she was still the only person
that cleaned that entire building—bragging about how smart her
grandchildren were—products of that school board's actions.

Clouds of milk in her coffee.
My grandmother's cup, though
decorated with lilies, was crafted
from clay. And everyone knew then
that porcelain was better. In it,
coffee black with cumulus clouds of milk
that spread like foundations built on fine
features. Clouds of milk blossoming in rip-
ples of coffee, black no more.

Coffee clouds in milk, porcelain
marbled imperfect.

Vitiligo's mourning sip.

My fraternal grandmother, I don't know when she was born. She went into the ground as we ate breakfast in Williamsburg, Virginia—a weekend shopping getaway. My father had an attitude the whole time. His mother had died and he was trying not to grieve for a woman who only wished ruin upon him. I don't know much about her, but I know she cleaned the Northumberland County courthouse when she wasn't pimping out her own daughters for money to spend on fashions from the Sears, Roebuck catalogue. My father stills doesn't eat cabbage, because it reminds him of all the watery soups he consumed as a child, as his mother twirled in fur coats before a chipped mirror in a house with no plumbing. His father either out on the fishing boat working, laying asphalt in DC during the humid summers, or too drunk to notice the neglect.

Dad grew up in the country, where his mother moved furniture often.

Recollects moments when she said *Stand there, let me look at you, you look sharp.*

Remembers when she pulled furniture from the walls and corners to clean.

"She knew how to turn neck bones into a meal; mashed potatoes into pancakes the next morning."
She said "*Snakes gets comfortable in dark places.*"

In the south, move your furniture
when you clean. Don't let it
stand there, be sharp.

Her own mother taught her
during that time when black homes
weren't made of brick and stone,
sealed with cement.

Rickety foundations, like missing branches
in trees, welcome snakes
like a garden with no gate.

Old Orlean was a witch from the Village of Reeds
she birthed six daughters of seven seeds
my father was the junior that game me his seniors name
but my father from his mother carries a deepened shame

Old Orlean gave her red confections
to men with erections that have her adoration
and pretty things

whilst her husband was fishing the seas
making money for his family's needs

Money that Old Orlean was spending on empty stomachs,
scraped chicken backs, emptied bologna packs, and mohair slacks
in her size only. while my father and his sisters had to improvise
to disguise the holes in their clothes and ignore the taunts of others

and when money was a lack
she made her daughters pick up the slack
because who's a better madame than a mother
and what's a greater lesson in life than
that one suffers

The fear of the black mother manifest in tangible shadows that pull children into the water.

The fear of the black mother cannot swim because a white crow and polio kept her from square blue pools filled with round blue eyes.

The fear of the black mother is passed down like the story of Abel is told to white children at bedtime.

The fear of the black mother is the boogeyman stealing your children when her back is turned.

Nightmares of the Atlanta Child Murders,
knowing the real killers were those ghosts
in white robes that no one can touch.

You may have prayer and belief to
ward off those presences from the past,
but not even time can prepare you
for the crosses that you cannot leave
your front door to extinguish.

The fear of the black mother is a prayer that never ends, in the back of her mind, and under her breath whenever her children are not in her line of vision.

The fear of the black mother ignores Halloween and makes her children stay in the house.

The fear of the black mother still sends her child through barbed doorways in order to grow. Keeping band-aids in stock and hoping her kids only return home with nicks she can handle--wounds that she can kiss away.

There is a trauma that haunts black mothers as beloved as 124.[6]

The fear of the black mother is a coffin made from the wood of saplings, watching it lower into the ground.

The fear of the black mother is her own coffin going into the ground before her children are taught to cope in the black skin that she has bestowed.

Like a tree in an orchard with no rights
to the fruit plucked for the nourishment of others.
Shackled and watching the picking is a phobia
passed down like a recipe for pound cake.

The fear of the black mother is knowing her child will be seen for their blackness and not all of the color she taught them before kindergarten.

The fear of the black mother's questions the Cs amongst the As.
The black mother fears the whitewashing. The erasure of everything she has given them. The eradication of
their grandmother's tongue.

The fear of the black woman is that one day her stomach will grow with a life she has no power to sustain.

---

[6] The home address of Sethe from Toni Morrison's *Beloved*. The 124 is pivotal because of the missing three, that represents the child Sethe killed to spare from a life of enslavement and rape.

My father went to grade school with the coach's boys. They were my father's bullies. They made fun of him because of his mother, because she cleaned the courthouse, and because on occasion, my father had to go and help her. There's a rumor that one of my aunts tied my father and his bullies together—three children that look like the coach and one of them black.

My father parted ways with them after graduation to attend an HBCU[7], but was reconnected with one of them at the country club law school that accepted him as one of their first black students.

My father met my mother while she was working at legal services. It was mother's first desk job, after retail. She was an artist on her way to art school, but got pregnant out of wedlock. The lawyer married the artist, and they had two more kids.

My father is still one of the few black attorneys in my hometown with the longevity of his practice, and along the way he got a Masters in Divinity and became a pastor. So my sisters and I were fed morals and ethics from him, and imagination from my mother.

Cs were not accepted in my household, Bs had to be explained, and college was a definite. Odyssey of the Mind molded me—it's where I first discovered my love for writing stories. The greatest offense on my record is a speeding ticket I got because I was late to class.

My parents wanted to steer themselves from the mistakes made from a generation birthed from the reconstruction, steer us from the mistakes made by a generation used to spark the Civil Rights

[7] Historically Black College and University

Movement. I was taught to smile, though my parents shed many
tears.

However, will you
know any of this—
my appearance
how great my smile,
how distinguished

'til it

brings you pause
causes you
to cross the street.

For hundreds of years (and still), we were made
to darken in the sun,

then left to pale.

Say the phrase "you live and you learn"
out loud,

now say "it does not apply to black people"
out loud.

Now do you feel the movement? We never wanted
our closed eyes to be met with gnashing teeth.

We only wanted the empathy from those that, too,
sucked milk from our mother's breast.

We only wanted to be black and beautiful in a land
that told us black was everything but, and still we are
black and beautiful,

raising within the sun.

in the way you graze my skin
you tell me. in the way you ig-
nore my possessed, in the way
you take me, and still i stand—
still,

you reign my function, name
removed. you. this body is not.
yours, this flesh
is not a shield.
it can be pierced
and i can pour out,
warm to cold,
warm to cold,

warm too

cold puddle on the concrete, that
body is no longer a me,
but me does not exist any-
more, me did not exist before. i,

the body is not mine. was not
mine. to a possessive pronoun i
belonged to the body that takes me
from my. i belong to the body. i.

i.
i.

me.

this.
that.

Them.

I like playing tennis. There is something about the volley that I take personally, and something about losing the rhythm of that volley that makes the sky and world feel like they are falling in some undefined motion downward. Being the person that interrupts a good volley is a feeling of not belonging where you stand.

I went to tennis camp one summer; it was not a sleep away camp, just a day camp—well an early morning camp—at Kenmore Park downtown—the park named after Betty Washington—George's sister.

I was a growing boy, and by growing I mean overweight for my age. I don't remember feeling my weight, but it was easy to tell that I ate more and got less exercise than my peers. However, I was fast. I could run fast, but asthmatic lungs caused me to fall to last place very quickly. I could start a mile run during gym class, and at tennis camp, in the lead, but then I would slow down to a walk for the remainder of those miles around the athletic fields and those jogs around the tennis courts.

I like playing tennis. My dad started playing tennis in college on courts named after Richmond, Virginia's own Arthur Ashe, until his aging knees kept him from those clay and hard top tennis courts. He passed, at least, an interest of the sport to my sisters and me.

I was a big boy. The type of kid that other parents called handsome, stocky, sturdy, and probably the worse away from the ears of my mother. I was buoyant in my deluded ability to play tennis, because my father was so adept to the sport. I was a big boy. I was often teased for it, so I had to show out when I could. I had to run fast until I couldn't. In my head I had to go the extra mile not to appear sloppy in appearance—because that what the world told me I was—

sloppy. I was a big boy, but I was still a boy and my confidence was non-existent (and to be honest it only shows up on occasion now). I am a growing

man. I wanted to grow into a man once,
back when I thought the utterance of my fem-
ininity was a insult.

I now want to be a person,
continue to grow.

I had a single best friend one time. We met in the fourth grade. We had the same homeroom teacher. He thought I was cool for some reason. I don't know why. Maybe it was because I felt the need to make the class laugh so that they were not laughing at me, but with me. I did not share my best friend's interest in sports—which were a big part of his personhood—especially football. I tried to collect football cards once, but I assumed all of the glossy cards were of good players. I was horribly wrong.

He and I liked to stay up late at night during weekend sleepovers, scaring the shit out of ourselves with horror movies and ghost stories. He lived within walking distance of our middle school, and on lucky days I was able to walk home with him, hanging out, and not doing homework until my mother picked me up from his house.

We used to saunter to his house looking for some sort of adventure that would keep us outdoors longer. We always drifted towards water—hoping for frogs, newts, and other life forms that thrived in streams.

The tennis courts stood next to a dangling chain that separated the schoolyard from the very street on which my friend lived. There were four of them—hard courts with verdant weeds growing through the cracks of their faded emerald tops. I don't think we ever had a tennis unit in any of the physical education classes that I took at that school, and I cannot recall if there was even a competitive division for middle school tennis—thus the courts were unkempt flatlands in front of the water tower.

I did not know the girls, but he did. I recognized their faces from passing them in the hallways, but I did not know them. I did not know their names. They were standing on the courts, with their rackets, and a ball. He wondered if they would let us play. He asked if we could play. Their rackets fell to theirs sides and their free hands took rest on their hips.

Mouths opened.

You can, but not that *nigger*.

I felt as if I was called fat and a faggot all at once, as if a dog was biting and ripping me away at the knees, and I did not know what part of me to protect. I did not know which part of me was showing that I needed to hide. I did not know where the dis-ease was.

Lowering my voice or covering my boy boobs or checking the limpness in my wrist was not going to save me from that situation. It was the first time I had heard the word as a dagger with 'er'. The blond girl said it first, then the brunette with pigtails.

I responded silently with the only privilege I had—the fact that my father was a lawyer, the fact that I lived in a middle class subdivision, the fact that my father had a law office and a home within walking distance from where we stood; but that did not stop the insults. That did not prevent the first time I was called a nigger. Just like being in law school did not stop my father from being called one. I was nothing more than an insult to these girls, and social class was not going to save me from the offense that was embedded in the melanin of my skin.

What happens to the body
when it is emptied of its record?

Does it crack and dust over
like a reservoir that has gone dry, waiting for
rains to ease chapped mud?

What happens to the flesh
when the muscle atrophies from
a diet of sticks and stones?

What happens to the bones
when the marrow is forgotten?

What happens to the body
when the branch snaps, and no one
is around to hear it?

What happens to the body
after it is first called *nigger*?

Awareness happens to the *nigger*.[8]

We walked to my childhood friend's house in silence. His mother saw that I was upset, he told her what happened, and my mother was called to pick me up. I was spoken to about the word, even though I knew it was tied to my appearance—at that age every insult was linked to my appearance. When I was first called a faggot, I retaliated with, "I ain't fat." I thought I heard the word with two Ts and not Gs.

It is funny how our ears turn the whispers of others into our own insecurities.

The older, blonde girl apologized to me as I sat in the main office of school on the day following the accost with the word. I was sent to the office because I was giving my homeroom teacher an exceptionally hard time being the class clown, so when my pencil slipped from my grip mid-swing of a goofy walk towards her desk, and landed close to her body, she took it as me throwing the pencil at her, and I was sent to the office.

I was already terrified of having to hear the disappointment in my mother's voice and the anger in my father's after school, so when she walked into the office it was no surprise that I wanted to burst into tears.

She apologized to me through a raspy and ashamed voice, but even after her apology I could not help but to always notice her and her

---

[8] Frequency illusion, also known as the Baader-Meinhof Phenomenon, is defined as a singularity in which people learn or notice something for the first time and begin to see it everywhere.

accomplice every time I passed them in halls—every time they were in close proximity to my body. When they played field hockey with my sister. When we were in the same gymnasium for pep rallies, and when they cheered at football games. Even as adults, when they cashed and deposited my checks at the bank, and purchased pizza from me at Wegman's. I would recognize them—the aged faces of those two little girls who introduced me to the word.

The haunt is what happens to the body.

My childhood friend and I remained associates for some years after that incident; however, our rise into our teens dissolved the feigned brotherhood.

After I got my license, I drove to his house to find he'd moved away. The last time I'd been there I was 14, thinking it was going to be like old times, and the whole time we fought about music. I was falling in love with rhythm and blues and funk, and he was all about the dichotomies of rap and country. When I pulled into the driveway, that day at 16, I ignored the 'for sale' sign, and no one answered the door.

He sent me a *friend request* twice within a decade of one another. Once to catch up, defriending me somewhere between my rampant support of a black president and the eye-opening death of Trayvon Martin (did I mention he lived in Florida?), and secondly, to tell me about the passing of his father and then defriended me again somewhere between my posts about the angering and heartbreaking murder of Eric Garner and the rage and horror that was evoked by the murder of Sandra Bland. I never defriended him, but I did unfollow him for his outlandish remarks against our then "non-Christian, socialist President", and his post about "not really knowing" what happened between Trayvon's murderer and Trayvon.

The defriending became a whisper
that turned into those words
both with double Gs in the middle.

Though I continuously get called a faggot, I haven't been directly called a nigger since, but I have filled spaces with it. Syllabi without writers of color. A customer that demanded I thank him for buying a pizza that I made. A teacher telling me that I should not write about race, or even the teacher that wanted me to make my grandmother more "ethnic" and "boisterous" in a piece I wrote for an undergrad non-fiction class.

I hear it when people steer away from my body in predominantly white neighborhoods, and when looked at with a gaze of suspicion. I hear it every time the death of a black body is displayed in the news and no remorse is given to it. I hear it when black women are called sassy, and black boys are called *thugs*. I hear it whenever the conversation is about Michael Vick, and not about the rapist on the team. I hear it when Obama is referred to as the worst president ever.

I heard it when I was the only black student in classrooms. I heard it when I was the only person put into handcuffs out of a group that smelled like marijuana.

I hear it every time my students (of all races) use the word as misnomer for man or person, or as a synecdoche of themselves. I heard when I was confused for a student and not an adjunct—when a coworker at the college where I used to work at asked me where'd *I* get my keys, and why was *I* using the faculty bathroom?

I hear it every day when get I on the 580—looking at the green hills to the east and the concrete jumble to the west.

I have not picked up a racket in years, but I get the urge every summer when televisions around me find themselves catching glimpses of Serena. Every year it makes me wistful of those few moments when I found myself in a perfect volley with a competitor. Those few times when I felt I had something to offer to the sport, and it makes me want to purchase a new racket to take up the sport in California, but then I remember I have asthma, and there are a few attacks I don't want to relive.

FEAR

We go way back—back to those nights when you slept with the closet light on—those nights when you avoided looking down the pitch dark hallway while everyone slept—avoiding the phantom phantoms—those nights when you loved the fact that your father was an insomniac, because he kept the lights on around the house—those nights when the same closet lights that helped you sleep introduced you to shadows of hanging clothes that roused your fear more than the encapsulation of darkness.

We go back to those days when you faked sick to avoid *hey yo' faggot* and wanting to stand last in line. Those days when you knew you were looking at boys more than girls, and you knew it would introduce your parents to a shame—a dis-ease—that you feared more than the witch that used to lay on you.

We go back to your silence. The days when the answer to "how was your day?" was always "fine", because parents don't want to hear that their son got called "faggot" more than his given name. We go back to those days when you knew the answer in class, but did not want your voice heard by those boys that called it *girly*—all of the "I don't knows" when you really did know. I stole your voice—I steal it now.

We go back to that day when those blond pigtails called you *nigger*, and made you realize at an early age what hate was, what the Confederate flag meant, and that not all country smiles came from hearts as sweet as tea.

I permeate the south. I instituted the south.

You drove blacks
to the north—
to cities to choke
on coal and soot.

Drove me
from my home,
and I found you
under every step
that I took.

Wide eyes walking
from the quandaries
of plantations,
into the open
season of their
ruin.

Given a wasteland
that smelled like the charred
missing branches of
trees.

What fruit can we grow here?
What stone will it hold?
Its too heavy for the soil.

A singe wafting
through centuries
a taste breasted
in the milk.

We go back to those days when you changed out of your pink shirt and amethyst gauges before you drove into Caroline County— where the Lovings found love. Those days when you snuck around with your sexuality in that deep pocket with the zipper, hid your boyfriends, hid your lube—in the mind of a closeted 19-year-old, only faggots use lube.

Distance and darkness
are all a gay man needs
to silence the voices in
his head,

        until the holidays
        riding those trains
        back south.

We go back to that feeling you got in Philly, when those homies called you soft and you thought you were. Not yet recognizing the power of the feminine that you possess. It was the envy and fear of the womb that birthed misogyny and patriarchy and sexism—the prototype for the anaphora of divisions that followed.

All of the dis-eases.

I have this theory:

sex was the darkness'
first success,
full attempt at chaos.

In every book, those two
made of earth and water.

Sediments of filth
and the solution to its
removal.

Sickly-sweet sap
flowing from caning
our backs

divided
crystal from
molasses.

We go back to those days when thinking about your steps faltered your walk. When thinking about your voice made it uncertain. Those days when the baseball coach begged you to be on the team that laughed when you showed up to practice—he called you one of the best hitters he'd ever seen and you let those swings die—because as you know, we go back.

You remembered me through that triumphant moment in the locker room when everyone silenced themselves and questioned your presence.

You hit better than all of them, and you only showed them once, because I stopped you.

You could've been more, but I stopped you from wanting.

I stopped you from reaching. I kept you from looking into all of those white faces at the University of Virginia. I put that weed in your first blunt, and you got stuck for seven years, three universities and no degree.

We go back to those nights in George Washington and Jefferson National Forest when you feared white faces more than the wolves howling in the distance. Those days when you wanted to go hiking in Shenandoah, but feared the dwellers of the valley— inherited fear. I'm post-traumatic now.

We go back to that year when we shared a studio apartment in Los Angeles. We drank bottles of Bulleit Bourbon alone. You fried enough chicken for the both of us, but only you ate it. We grew together in Los Angeles, and I told you how ugly you were amongst all of those beautiful faces of West Hollywood.

We spent whole weekends together on the futon with six packs, whiskey, weed and food, and we grew together in that studio with roaches the size of mice, and that window with the alley view that made every day seem gloomy.

We imagined rainy days, and stayed dry.

We chose not to discover that place, and we choose not to discover new places still. Remember those stares at Sea Ranch, in Santa Monica, in Walnut Creek? They were not imagined.

We go back to those days when you did not want to be seen. To the days when you don't want to be seen now. Those days when your students remind you of the voices that silenced your own in grade school. Those days when you go back to Virginia to visit your mother, and you stay in the house, avoiding eyes that only see a black man due to their lack of empathy. Black mothers go without sympathy, they have never stopped singing.

for black men, they have never stopped crying for themselves—Miss Celie taught you that. Avoiding good ol' boys, those with badges and those without, those with and without masks.

I am the doubt
that pokes holes
in your confidence,
then points them out

to the world.

We go back.

Unlike your parents, your siblings, your friends, I will be here with you until the darkness surrounds you and drowns you. Remember when I kept you from learning to swim? Kept you from taking your clothes off in front of others? Kept you from loving yourself?

We go back.
You and me.

We go
back.

I am
here
for
you.

BATTLE HYMN

I walked past Ricky Battle's red house today, on accident. The entirety of the day felt like an early evening, as if I'd slept in too long. I was on the way to another friend's house to see his new place, smoke, and catch up. I had never walked within or into that particular part of Oakland before, but I have admired it from the windows of the #31 bus route. It's a photogenic amalgam of art and industry at the western-most edge of Oakland. Where the bay breathes engine exhaust and exhales sea salt—where warehouse are exorcised into million-dollar condos.

The red house stood out—stood out as a memory—I didn't realize it was his from a distance, but when I saw the gated door and remembered walking through it, I realized that it was Ricky B's. I had only been once.

He messaged me on Facebook one Saturday during my first year in Oakland—my year of homesickness and gray depression. Funny thing is he recognized me from a dating site back when we both lived in and around DC, and then recognized me again, on the same dating site, in the Bay Area. I knew what that dating site was for and gave him my Facebook link, to parlay the courtship into friendship. We spoke here and there via direct message and eventually started texting.

He messaged one Saturday night and said:

My house is full of people from the DMV (DC, Virginia, and Maryland) and you need to be here.

We had spoken online for months, planned to meet several times, and each time my fortress-like room took over my abilities to leave it. Leaving my house when I first moved to Oakland, for things that did not pertain to grad school, was difficult. Even when I did find myself in bars it was usually with classmates.

Ricky was the first, and only, friend I met in the Bay Area that I did not know through the writing world, academia, and the spaces in which those two realms merged; and he introduced me to others who had found their way to California from the suburbs of the nation's capital.

He picked me up alone, and he gave me the rundown of the people at his house. All graduates of Duke Ellington School for the Arts, and all working within some sector of the art world.

Even at night I could tell that the house was red from the sole exposed lit light bulb inside of the gated portico. It used to be an old storefront turned studio apartment—in Dogtown—a village in Oakland where the art is in the very streets.

The first thing I noticed about the colorful interior of his home was the one tall wall painted with chalkboard paint. It was covered with his writing plans, goals, and more plans. More plans than I had ever made in different colors of chalk, each representing a level of completeness. Since meeting him I learned that W.E. B. Du Bois had made plans for himself up until his 120th birthday, and he lived until he was 95—I heard this from Amiri Baraka's own lips two years before he died. The lesson from that being to make plans and never stop, and maybe death will turn its head on your aging body until you have gotten enough of them done—but *enough* clearly is not the same for everyone.

One of Ricky's projects was a novel, and it was during that conversation, I found out he did not limit himself to the title of writer—just always wanted to write a novel, so he did.
A seed of jealousy was planted when he told me that it was almost complete. Here I was standing in front of a self-made event planner and promoter, writer, producer, and manager of up-and-coming musicians. He was everything I once saw myself as before I fell into the writing program, and he was even a better writer than me because he had self-discipline. Here I was, letting days come and go, without ever picking up a pen, except to do class assignments

I was not writer, I was barely a student.

But it was when he said that he was also a Big Brother that I knew I was sitting in the room with James Baldwin, or W.E.B. Du Bois himself, and I was never going to be as great as him.

I fell in love with the wrong guy when I first ventured to the Bay Area. He was in my writing program and everything I thought I wanted physically in a person. I'm one to live in fairy tales, so when he contacted me, I accepted his friend request. I knew we were going to get married and have a slew of adopted babies and be happy. We woke up together a few times. I went out with him for Halloween in the Castro. I did not want to go, but he mentioned it several times through the day on campus. Somewhere after workshops and the after-class drinks, I agreed to go.

It was a Thursday—a school night—Halloween—and by the second time I saw him make out with another random guy, I felt how early I had to wake up in the morning. As I headed to the door of the bar, I anticipated the walk to MUNI, the transfer to BART, and my two-mile walk through West Oakland from the station. My feet already yearned for the couch fold in my futon. Not to mention, my heart, which was simultaneously numbing itself to the loneliness of promiscuity with every step I took through the crowd of masked men.

I freed myself from the bar and ventured into the crowded and masqueraded streets. At the precipice of my emotion I looked up from my steps and stared into the face of Tim Burton's Mad Hatter, and he spoke to me;

it was Ricky B.

I did not say hello, I just asked him what he was doing—and I hoped he was going home—and he was—and he gave me a ride—scolding me the entire way for not hanging out with him more. We talked about how I shared the same birthday as his deceased mother, one of his best friends and three of his exes—seemed like a work of the fates. I got out his car with the promise of seeing him again, and soon—the fates were going to make it happen

It was a Sunday morning, and my black curtains were drawn, when I got a direct message from a friend that I met through Ricky B. When she firstly said hello, I knew it wasn't a greeting of candor, even with the absence of her voice, I knew this was not easy for her. When she said hello, I knew the sky was gray without even having to open my curtains.

I turned on my space heater with my foot.

Ricky had moved to Miami two months prior to this Sunday morning message. I remember him initially telling me online about his departure from the bay, and me being upset. Why move back to the south? And to the state that killed Trayvon? He said it was the right time to be a promoter in Miami.

Who was I to talk him into staying? He was constantly trying to get me to leave my house, and I was constantly giving him excuses, and who was I to talk him out of it—even though there was a selfish piece of me that felt safer in the Bay knowing that he was a call and a five-minute drive from my house. We ended the conversation with me promising to go to his "going away" happy hour party.

But, I remember letting drinks with my classmates get out of hand, hoping to wake up in my classmate's bed in the Castro, and going straight home disappointed in an early, pre-10 pm pass-out drunk state, texting Ricky the next morning as he began his journey east, and telling him that we were bound to see each other again—we were both from the DMV.

The direct message said, "Did you hear about Ricky?"

"No, what happened?" I had already pulled up his Facebook page and seen the farewells, and prayers, noticed all the periods at the end of the sentences; but I still needed her to tell me.

She responded, "He died this morning."

After reading that, I found myself in my room blocking out the sun. I closed my eyes hoping for sleep to promote stagnancy, and only saw the list of plans drawn in colorful chalk in the darkness of my closed eyes. I heard him scolding me about not hanging out. And I got out of bed and opened my curtains: the day was not gloomy.

When I found myself museless, I hear his impassioned voice talking about volunteering, so I volunteered in schools for the rest of my time in grad school. Volunteer work that allowed me to get my foot in the door for teaching—teaching inspires my writing, constantly, and writing is constantly reminding me that I have stories yet to experience.

Don't let 'em die.

I won't let him die ...

The beast of the sea sips tea with the loud-
est persons in the room, shoveled dirt over

his own grave to ignore death. He slithers
into his own mouth, where perdition suppurates,

and spits into the mouths of the thirsty, and
they drink, ignoring the rimes of the ancient.

madres latinas que encienden
velas a Eshu like black mothers
kneel and pray to Jesus brown
y negro boys muertos en la calle

do pulled pork and ham
break down the same in the gut?

does one blacken and dis-
solve, as the other is glori-
fied in the throat.

the moat around the king-
dom is molten.

heart
burn.

BLACK SUITE

ATTACK ON WATA

(notes on June 6ᵗʰ, 2015)

Black bodies integrating that once un-bodied water and the sharks
screamed, "Polio, where's the bleach?" We thought they feared water
because it is where we stole them from themselves, put them on
ships, before the beauty of blue eyes was instilled and buried deeper
than the orishas that were buried in the sand, which had eroded
away on the ships that slashed the artery from the heart of the world.

Officer Casebolt knew that the 14-year-old Dajerria Becton was
really Mami Wata in disguise; he saw her innocence for the bole of
the serpent. Mistook her free-running mouth for something that
needed to be silenced with an iron bit. Mistook her fragile spine
for the theoretical adamantium spine of Freddie Gray. Mistook her
exposed skin for promiscuity and desired to touch her like King
Kong wanted Ann Darrow. He saw her for everything that Africa
is and he wanted its resources like the drooling mouths of France,
England, and China.

Can we talk about the pleasures he felt as he drilled his knee into
her back? Can we get to the root of the sexual violence done to black
female bodies? Can we not forget to #sayhername because we are
distracted by the deaths of all of the men. Why are we so distracted
with death? Is this freedom? Why does the reconstruction have an
end date, when the trauma is still haunting us, the wound is still
open and there ain't shit strange about the fruit anymore?

America has given blacks
reason to sing spirituals,
but wants us to forget why

chariots had to swing low.

We sang "Oh, Happy Day"
even after Emmett was tilled,
and those four girls were reduced
to ash.

"Precious Lord" at the tombing
of the King.

"I believe I Can Fly" for Trayvon.

Orishas are still getting replaced with dogma that makes us believe
that because Mami Wata was known for her snakes, she was evil.
But she was no gorgon, nor a Lillith. She wasn't a whore. She was the
Mother to the world. A mother like Leslie MacSpadden and Mamie
Till, who both screamed, waking us up, telling us to "look at what
the world did to my baby."
Black women have never stopped singing
for black men.

Black women have never stopped crying
for themselves. Shug Avery taught me that.
Assata taught me that. Maya Angelou. Angela
Davis. Miss Celie.

Sista, you've been on my mind.

So many tombstones, marches, murders
and hashtags for a movement that never stops
moving—can't afford to stop.

Great grand mothers, grandmothers, wives, mothers, aunts, sisters, and daughters crying for:

Eric Garner
Walter Scott
Darrien Hunt
Tamir Rice
Philando Castille
Freddie Gray
Keith Lamont Scott
Terence Crutcher
...

#somanyblackboysandmenkilledbycopsthatIhavetroublekeepingup
withallofthenames

Casebolt saw Dajerria's body for the sons that she could produce, and like Ellen Ripley he knew to stop the horde. He had to go for the queen. He wanted to spare her the eulogizing hum of the mourning Black Mother.

CRIES FROM THE LION'S DEN

(more notes on June 6th, 2015)

Have you ever heard one of those voices that just broke your heart?
It was not exactly the sounds and words and phrases coming out
of the person's mouth that saddened you, even though they did, it
was more the person's timbre, their vibration, their resonance, that
gave you that single paining heartbeat, and made you want to cross
any boundaries to embrace them and do whatever you could to take
their pain away.

We live in a wicked, wicked world where a black 16-year-old boy is
the equivalent of the "Son of Sam", who took six lives, and the man
who shot John Lennon. Where a 16-year-old boy served the full
three years that were initially given to Sonny Rollins.

After ten months, Sonny was playing jazz again, but Kalief Browder
remained in Rikers for three years. And two of those years were
spent in solitary confinement. All because he never stopped
professing his innocence. All because he never stopped singing for
himself—singing about trees in a cage.

He never stopped running
from the dogs that were gnawing
at his knees—slept on southern
cotton sheets.

Instill the image of someone you love who is Kalief's age. Imagine
them in jail, never having been to prom; never having done anything
wrong.

In an interview Kalief mentioned that he spoke to himself, and as he spoke he began to cry. He said people looked at him as though he were crazy—on the bus, on the train. He spoke to himself, figuring out life's problems out loud. "They don't know that for two years I sat in a cell all alone," he said through tears. Maybe he thought that if he could peel away the yellow paint from the gray walls, he would be free.

Imprisonment without evidence. The guilt of skin. The assumptions, the growths in minds of those that hate his skin.

During Black History Month, 2012,
he cut his white bed sheets into yarn, wrapped
them into strands, pulled the rope from
the master's hands, tried to take the reigns
of his own life,

but that little light of his broke in the dark-
ness of his lonely bird cage, and he lived on as that
crazy boy that sang the song of innocence to a justice
that was more than blind—or maybe it
was just deaf on the day of his arrest.

In 2013, during the month of thanks and giving,
and after freedom was given back to the bird, he tried
to clip his wings again, from the bannister in his
parents' home.

Three years of asking why made his life feel
like an unanswered question. Freedom came with
southern horrors imbedded in his brain—*do you*

even trust yourself after two years of forced solitude?

No one listens to the *I didn't do its* of someone
in solitary confinement. A trial that doesn't happen feels like a
sacrificial burning, but trials these days burn bodies after they've been
hanged just like they used to in the Jim Crow trading cards.

What is the price of three years stolen, beginning at age 16?

He succeeded in clipping his wings
the third time with an air
conditioning power chord.

We can only eulogize what he could've been,
he only could've flown from the ground,
there isn't a rapsheet to discolor his wings.

There wasn't ever one to begin with.

FIRE NEXT TIME

(notes on June 17th, 2015)

Attacks on black churches are nothing new.

I remember in the late '90s, when my father started his own journey
to becoming a pastor. He was from a rural town where the mouth
of the Tappahannock River met the Chesapeake Bay—a peninsula,
because another river, the Rappahannock had a mouth that yawned
just on the southern side of him. His journey into the clergy took us
back to regions where people knew him as a boy, to revivals in the
dead of night, in corn and wheat fields so dark that the church had
to be heaven in my adolescent mind.

There were a string of arson attacks on black churches during this
time, so I remember sitting in the church, afraid of the Devil, yes,
but afraid he was going to seek his revenge on God through his
or her worshippers, and seek it then and now. The choir would be
singing

It was just a shabby ole place
Where we used to sing Amazing Grace
We used to have a good time, oh Lord,
Talkin' 'bout a real good time.

And I would be sitting in the pew expecting smoke and heat to rise,
and doors to be barred shut against the screams of the devoted.

This is the religion forced upon us
when ours was deemed witchcraft,
polytheistic and for the savage.

Now *the savage* burns us during prayer time
but the savage is just misunderstood and lonely
with a past of being quiet.

They turned 16th Street Baptist into a brick oven
that roasted four little girls* beyond the recognition
of their parents, beyond the ability to hear choirs sing again;

made the government

pass the Church Arson Prevention Act
during the civil rights movement;

made Clinton create
the National Church Arson Task Force
in the '90s;
made this happen after they enslaved
us in dogma, then freed us to the demons,
freed us to black codes, Jim Crow, and
black on black crime.

Now they want to tell us that the demons
suffer from themselves. That wolves are not wolves,
and we keep singing, "Oh, Happy Day."

We never suffer from ourselves,
we create suffering and uncomfortable
remembrance that causes our flesh to be
forever guilty of revenge.

We just keep singing, "Oh, happy day,"
hoping we'll sprout wings while the wolves
gnaw at our feet. Who needs feet with wings?

Who needs to land in heaven?

Heaven has no stones.

It used to be a shabby old place,
where we believed in amazing grace...
We used to...

Oh Lord...

We used to...

In real life,
the Baltimore P.D.
lynched Freddie Gray
without a tree
or a noose.

In the news, however,
Freddie was a magical negro,
like John Coffey.

He became his own tree
and his own noose.

Magic.

Magic like the dope
that grows next to liquor
stores.

Magic like the highways
that divide right
from wrong.
Magic like the ghosts
when they first stepped
onto native land.

Magic like the his-
stories that convinced us
darkies that we were
thieves.

Magic like the leaves
that continue to grow
from charred branches.

Magic like the ability
to walk away from
and ignore fault.

Magic like the evolution
of nigger to thug.

Magic like Cheikh
Anta Diop's Two Cradle
theory.[9]

Magic like Ida B.
Wells finding unrest
in her grave.

Magic like the knock
on Mose Wright's door.
Magic like the bullet
that downed the King.

Magic like Sandra Bland
never making it to her dream.

---

[9] A theory that divides the world into two cradles: the northern cradle that had
poor weather and bad soil that cannot sustain the life that inhabits the region; and
the southern cradle that has ample resources for its inhabitants, because of great
weather and fertile soil. In order to survive the northern cradle must venture into the
southern cradle—they must colonize.

Magic like the application of (men)tal health.

Magic like authenticity of fake
guns in black hands.

Magic like how the black boy
is always a man.

Magic like the fear of standing
your ground.

Magic like white hoods evolving
to black uniforms with guns and the right
to end.

The magic to end
The magic to end
The magic to end

Magic.

OAKLAND

This is a city of BART stops. A city where the homie on the platform across from me smokes a bowl freely in the open while I write about him in my journal. A city wrapped in the suffocation of concrete bridges, connecting highways, striving ivy ignored for the dying grass and what it means.

This is a city where the whites police and survey the blacks while trickling into the homes of dead relatives. A place with rose gardens far from the pricks of needles. A city of liberals that only talk to the Obama type of brotha, if that.

A city where I don't look safe, even in my vest and tie, having just left a job that I had to get a lot of schooling for, be the only black person in a classroom for, smile when I wanted to rage out for. This is a city where I still feel my black skin for Oscar Grant when I thought I left that feeling in the south with Trayvon. Where I still feel my black skin for Reagan and crack, and blunts in the hand of 13 year olds.

This is the city and I rarely venture onto the bole of the water serpent on the other side of the bay, even Bayview is going blind to funk and scat of enjambment—losing its purpose to the Great Migrators who made it blue like their collars during the second great war.

A city with two black eyes on a beautiful face that still smiles defiantly, holding onto itself. This is a city where ignorance stares and opens its mouth like a child with a secret that cannot be kept, a city where Berkeley students swim into the murky depths or sink into a similitude of faces.

This city is the neo-Nazi brother to San Francisco, New Orleans, Detroit, St Louis, Atlanta, Baltimore, DC, Philadelphia, and many others in the pupa stage of racial cleansing. The reverse white flight, the reclamation of fear with nervous hands on sturdy guns that know the objective of their bullets, regardless of their wielder's distress.

This is a city with clear boundaries that one is not meant to cross until they are forced out like a parasite.

A city of broken sidewalks and dogs without leashes that only bark at black passersby. A city of guesses and assumptions. A city of silent Sundays with sparse streets, packed grocery stores, and houses for every belief. A house for every sin. A city of crosswalks and jaywalkers. A city of litterers and divine conservationists. A city where justice is spoken in terms of restoration, because it is a city where justice was taken.

This is a city where the stairwells stop, where the hills drop, and only the climber knows which way is up, and only a few are taught about the ledges that were meant to hold their weight.

Streetlights play no games
on flat streets where bumps
and humps halt the ones that
were never meant to get away—
babies having babies. Unpainted,
unmarked asphalt mesas in asphalt
deserts gnashing at the bottom of rusted out
cars. Kisses from the bay have only
been leaving salt these days. Succulence
replaces grass and we help it grow in pots.
A city where bus riders cover their mouths from
the sick of a homeless man eating rotten food
in a sun-soaked seat,[10] a city where the observer
wishes he had more than $7 to his name, so that he
could do more than just the right thing in classrooms
with rules that forget that books are not the only givers

of stories.

This bus is on fire
and the cause of my sweat
is never to blame.

tell the stories
of those with scars.

tales that were tracked
into prisons, those stories
that were tracked into
unplanned parenthoods.

tales that were tracked
into silence, like unfinished
murals under highways—
which have, on the other side,
residents who couldn't afford
to appreciate the aesthetics
of beauty, because class-
rooms told them they were ugly,

because the curriculum
didn't show them artists
who mirrored them, or the faces
of their ancestors—those *trade-
workers* in white-lined text
books.

walled-in chambers filled with bullets
that will never sprout the wings needed
from the back of those who long to climb
those hills.

tales that were quaked into
the fault of the asphalt, where it dried like tar
before the feathering.

Unspoken stories, the true meaning of
whitewashed. The bluest eyes, the hardest tries
to be everything.

The blackwashed,
caged crow, with no knowledge of lyrics
true to my learned experience.

California Carpenter Bees are black. I've been seeing a lot of them around my garden.

Pollinating the tomato flowers
waiting for the fuchsia to blossom.

They resemble Japanese beetles in flight, sun shining off their glossy exoskeletons.

They can easily be ignored for their lack of sunflower stripes, but they are collecting so much gold in their baskets.

Succulence creeps into flower
pots like crows after the seeds
of the blossoming sun.

There are fences around yards with gardens too full of fruit for one household. Empty Victorians, boarded up Victorians, *blackwashed* Victorians. Those same Victorians will soon be painted and given the title of Majestic Ladies. Telling the houses around them that the cult of true womanhood is still only afforded by the master's wife— the lady of the house.

California tells Carpenter Bees that they better not sting, even if they could, allows them to collect pollen as long as they do not keep it for themselves. Honey is stored in houses on hills where honey-suckle is a weed that strangles flowers that are not native to the lands of the Calafia.

Cash for Houses
that were once ignored

until they became
rouged and flipped in-
to their fair ladies.

Roses touch them now,
they don't feel no thorns.

They don't feel no rot from
the black mold that was re-
moved from them.

Queen Victorians with jewel-
patched-crowns.

Calafia's griffins with wings
clipped are swallowed by the tower-
ing concrete from
acorns of Constantinople.

When the son of Marie Laveau and Calafia was pierced in the side
by a bullet of man to who proclaimed through the air of the lower
bottoms, "You can kill my body, and you can take my life, but you
can never kill my soul. My soul will live forever!"

His body was planted in Evergreen Cemetery, and his soul thrives in
Oakland.

Killed by those
who needed
fruit the most,

in the mourning of empty

stomachs and deserts
where concrete grows
hot cheetos as breakfast
for the children.

Red die
my mind
keep it
caged in

Constant in opal.
Kill the legacies
of my mothers
replace the
narratives
of her suns.

Capitalism has a lot of trust in us.

It knows even through protest that we'll catch it if it falters
backwards.

Capitalism never worries about hitting the ground, because even
when our hands are calloused and cracked open we'll still catch it.
This relationship is not symbiotic. Capitalism will never catch us.
If we fall, it is because capitalism needs us to in order to keep itself
alive.

There is a disease in the land,
until we all stop trusting it.

A SOUTHERN RECIPE
FOR INNOCENTS

(Feeds Four Horsemen: Bobby Frank Cherry, Thomas Blanton,
Herman Frank Cash & Robert Chambliss)

Ingredients:

- 4 Innocents[10] (Three within 14 years of development: Addie Mae
  Collins, Carole Robertson, Cynthia Wesley. One within 11
  years: Denise McNair.)

- 19 Sticks of Dynamite (Set delay timer on oven to avoid the
  judgment of the anti-cannibal)

- 1 Stained-glass Window (Preferably depicting Christ leading
  little children, passion images may work, if Jesus is colored)

- 1 Unheard Sermon (The Love that Forgives)

---

[10] Signify: a small pheasant-like bird, flightless and imprisoned to the ground, made
to find homes in bushes, if daring think of a colored girl in her Sunday's best dress
that never made it home to eat her mother's Sunday meal.

Directions:

1   Preheat Byzantine brick-oven to 9, 032° Fahrenheit.

2   Marinate the four innocents in adopted scriptures, struction (decon- and/or re-), and unsung hymns.

3   Make sure the timer is set to alarm at 10:22 a.m. before ritual juices run blood.

4   After a blinding incandescence the innocents should be blackened beyond brown, but quite rare within.

5   Serve in the mourning that collects after the meat is cut and edict with just cause.

Dessert Suggestion: Rock throwers[11] prepared by the gunfire of just policemen (Virgil Ware: 13 & Johnny Robinson: 16)

---

[11] Signify: an invisible fish that has the ability to fly with an internal lung and gills, but has no defense from the tines of kites, if daring think of the most hated thing on the planet with a sweet tea and some candy.

ACKNOWLEDGMENTS

I have to thank God/the Universe/the Goodness in this world for continuing to guide my steps. My family for giving me all of the motivation needed to write this book. The first poet I ever knew, my sister, Monet (Keeve) Kay. The person who introduced me to hope, my sister, Shatema Lucas. My mother who never gave up on me, even when I had given up on myself—thank you for my spirit. My father, who showed me that people never stop growing and learning from their mistakes—and to add faults to my armor. My friends, who like my family, gave me so much motivation to get this done.

I also have to thank Nomadic Press, especially J.K. Fowler, for seeing purpose in my words, and being patient as I continued to gather ways of expressing myself. My editor, Michaela Mullin, for her unfathomable patience.

And, I'd like to thank myself, because I don't do it often enough.

Vernon Keeve III is a Virginia-born writer that California molded into an educator. He lives and teaches in Oakland. His purpose is to teach the next generation the importance of relaying their personal narratives, sharing their experiences, and taking control of their destinies.